23625

D0815474

811
Ang

STILL I RISE

NOV 2 0 2001		

DANVERS TWP. LIBRARY
105 South West Street
Danvers, Illinois 61732
Phone: 963-4269

Maya Angelou
Still I Rise

Art by Diego Rivera

Edited by Linda Sunshine

A Welcome Book

DANVERS TWP. LIBRARY
105 South West Street
Danvers, Illinois 61722
Phone: 963-4269

New York   Random House

You may write me down
in history
With your bitter,
twisted lies,

You may trod me
in the very dirt
But still, like dust,
I'll rise.

Does my sassiness
upset you?
Why are you beset
with gloom?

'Cause I walk
like I've got oil wells
Pumping in my
living room.

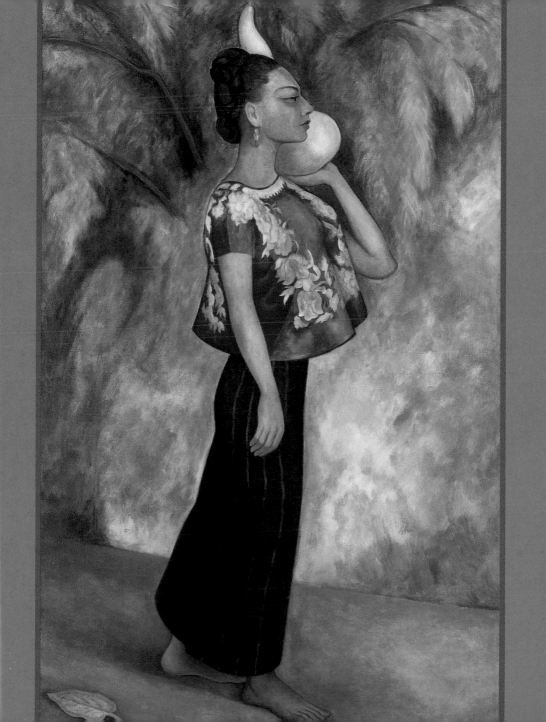

Just like moons
and like suns,
With the certainty
of tides,

Just like hopes
springing high,
Still
I'll rise.

Did you want
to see me broken?
Bowed head
and lowered eyes?

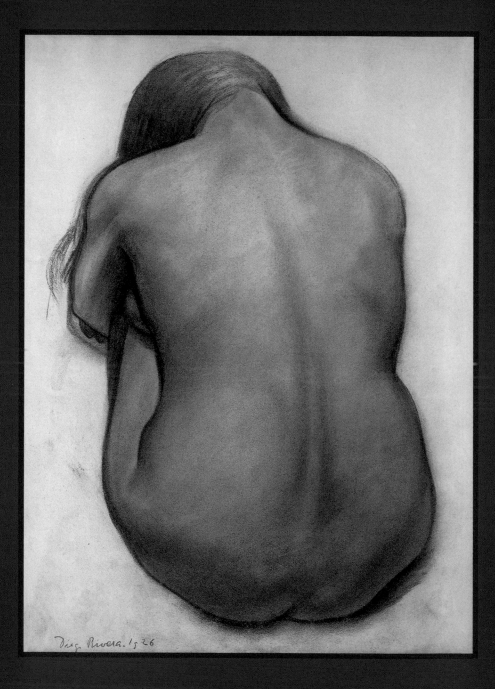

Shoulders
falling down
like teardrops,
Weakened by my
soulful cries.

Does my haughtiness offend you?
Don't you take it
awful hard

'Cause I laugh like I've got
gold mines
Diggin' in
my own backyard.

You may shoot me
with your words,
You may cut me
with your eyes,

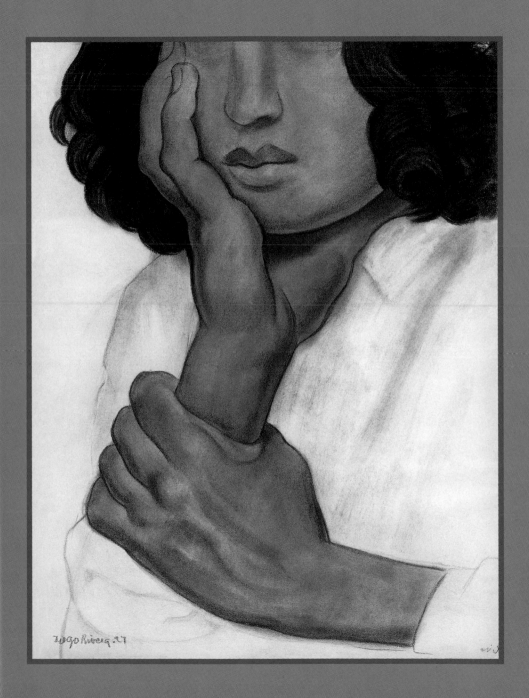

You may kill me
with your hatefulness,

But still,
like air,
I'll rise.

Does my sexiness upset you?
Does it come as a surprise

That I dance like I've got diamonds At the meeting of my thighs?

Out of the huts of history's shame **I rise**
Up from a past that's rooted in pain **I rise**

I'm a black ocean, leaping and wide, Welling and swelling I bear in the tide.

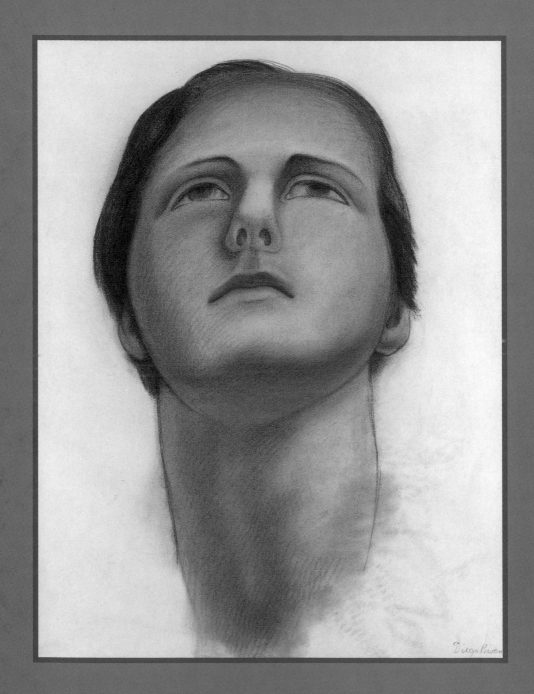

Leaving behind nights of terror and fear **I rise**
Into a daybreak that's wondrously clear **I rise**

Bringing the
gifts that my
ancestors gave,
I am the dream
and the hope of
the slave.

I rise

I rise

I rise.

Maya Angelou

"All of my work is meant to say, 'You may encounter many defeats but you must not be defeated.' In fact, the encountering may be the very experience which creates the vitality and the power to endure."

—As quoted in *The Norton Anthology of African American Literature*

She was born Marguerite Johnson on April 28, 1928, in St. Louis, Missouri, but her brother Bailey nicknamed her Maya ("mine"). Educated in Stamps, Arkansas, and San Francisco, California, she is a woman of rare talents and unprecedented accomplishments. Poet, writer, performer, teacher, and director, Maya Angelou is the author of the bestselling autobiographies *I Know Why the Caged Bird Sings* (nominated for a National Book Award), *Gather Together in My Name*, and *The Heart of a Woman*, as well as five collections of poetry and the poem "On the Pulse of Morning," which she read at the inauguration of President William Jefferson Clinton, the first African American and the first woman to be so honored. She has published two collections of essays and three children's books. She once said, "I write for the Black voice and for any ear which can hear it."

In theater, she produced, directed, and starred in *Cabaret for Freedom* in collaboration with Godfrey Cambridge at New York's Village Gate; starred in Genet's *The Blacks* at the St. Marks Playhouse; and adapted Sophocles' *Ajax*, which premiered at the Mark Taper Forum in Los Angeles in 1974. She wrote the original screenplay for the film *Georgia, Georgia*, and wrote and produced "Black, Blues, Black," a ten-part television series on African traditions in American life. She has appeared in numerous documentaries, feature films such as *How to Make an American Quilt,* and television shows, including *Roots* and *Touched by an Angel.* She has received many honorary degrees, is on the board of trustees of the American Film Institute, and is also one of the few female members of the Directors Guild. Fluent in English, Italian, Spanish, French, Arabic, and West African Fanti, she lectures frequently and contributes to many magazines and periodicals. She is the Reynolds Professor at Wake Forest University, Winston-Salem, North Carolina.

In 1998, she made her film directorial debut with Miramax's feature film *Down in the Delta.* For all these things and for the tender strength of her voice and vision, Maya Angelou is among the most respected and admired women in the world.

"I painted as naturally as I breathed, spoke or sweated."

—Diego Rivera

Born in December of 1886, Diego Rivera was drawing and painting by the age of three. "Almost as soon as my fat baby fingers could grasp a pencil, I was marking up walls, doors and furniture," he once told a journalist. He attended the National School of Fine Arts in Mexico City. In 1907, under government sponsorship, Rivera moved to Europe where he spent twelve years studying and painting with Picasso, Modigliani, and other artists who greatly influenced him. He returned to Mexico in 1921 and discovered his own style.

Enlisted by the government to create huge wall paintings, Rivera brought art to the people and reclaimed independent Mexican national culture. Eventually, his murals would cover the walls of schools, churches, hospitals, hotels, and government buildings in Mexico and in major cities in the United States.

He surrounded himself with strong-willed Marxist partisans and was committed to the ideals of communism. He fathered two daughters with his first wife, Lupe Marín. To support his family, he painted portraits of wealthy patrons and cannibalized his murals to make easel paintings and drawings, which he sold to Americans.

In 1928, he met Frida Kahlo, an exotic young beauty twenty years his junior. Hit by a bus as a teenager and gravely injured, Kahlo taught herself to paint during her long convalescence. Her relationship with Rivera was tumultuous. They married in 1929, divorced, and then remarried in 1940. Toward the end of her life, Kahlo said, "I had two accidents. One was a streetcar, the other was Diego."

On December 23, 1931, the Museum of Modern Art in New York City held a retrospective of 150 works by Rivera. Attended by more than 57,000 visitors, the show established Rivera as a pre-eminent artist.

Throughout his life, Rivera was a passionate collector of folk and pre-Columbian art. In the 1940s, he embarked on the idea of constructing a monumental building modeled on an Aztec pyramid. Today, that building houses his collection of 60,000 items from antique cultures.

Diego Rivera died on November 24, 1957, two years after the death of Frida Kahlo. Although he requested that his ashes be mingled with hers, he was instead interred in Mexico's Rotunda of Famous Men in the Civil Pantheon of Mourning. He is considered a national treasure of his native country.

Diego Rivera

Produced by Welcome Enterprises, Inc.
588 Broadway, New York, N.Y. 10012

Compilation copyright © 2001 by Welcome Enterprises, Inc.
"Still I Rise" copyright © 1978 by Maya Angelou
Illustrations copyright © 2000 Banco de México, Av. 5 de
Mayo No. 2, Col. Centro, 06059, México, D.F. Reproducción
autorizada por El Banco de México. Fiduciario en El
Fiedeicomiso relativo a Los Museos Diego Rivera y Frida
Kahlo. Reproducción autorizada por El Instituto Nacional de
Belles Artes y Literatura

All rights reserved under International and Pan-American
Copyright Conventions. Published in the United States by
Random House, Inc., New York, and simultaneously in
Canada by Random House of Canada Limited, Toronto.

RANDOM HOUSE and colophon are registered trademarks of
Random House, Inc.

Library of Congress Cataloging-in-Publication Data
Angelou, Maya.
    [And still I rise]
    Still I rise / Maya Angelou; edited by Linda Sunshine.
        p. cm.
    "A Welcome Book."
    ISBN 0-375-50596-2
1. Afro-Americans—Poetry. I. Sunshine, Linda. II. Title.

PS3551.N464 A8 2001
811'.54—dc21 00-045702

Random House website address: www.atrandom.com

Printed in Singapore on acid-free paper

9 8 7 6 5 4 3 2 1

First Edition

Edited by Linda Sunshine
A Greg/Clark Design

ILLUSTRATION CREDITS:

Front cover and page 29: *Mural Study for Chapingo (Woman with Two Children)*, 1927. Black and red crayon, 8 ^{11}/16 in. x 12 ^{5}/16 in. Philadelphia Museum of Art: Given by an anonymous donor. Photo by Lynn Rosenthal.

Back cover and page 26: *Nude with Calla Lilies*, 1944. Oil on masonite, 61 ^{13}/16 in. x 48 ^{13}/16 in. Collection of Emilia Gussy de Gálvez. Source: Biblioteca de las Artes (Archivo CENIDIAP/INBA). Centro Nacional de las Artes. México.

Page 2: *La Molendera (Tortilla Grinder)*, 1924. Oil on canvas 18 ^{1}/8 in. x 21 ^{5}/8 in. Courtesy of Mary-Anne Martin/Fine Art, New York.

Page 5: *Tehuana (Retrato de Columba Dominguez)*, 1950. Oil on canvas. 193 x 122 cms. Courtesy of Mary-Anne Martin/Fine Art, New York.

Pages 6–7: *Sunset*, 1956. Oil and tempura on canvas, 11 ^{7}/8 in. x 15 ^{3}/4 in. Fundacion Dolores Olmeda, Mexico City, D.F., Mexico. Credit: Schalkwijk/Art Resource, NY. Source: Art Resource: 65 Bleecker Street (9th fl.), New York, NY 10012.

Page 9: *Portrait of Enriqueta Davila*, 1949. Oil on canvas, 77 ^{3}/16 in. x 39 ^{3}/8 in. Colección: Enriqueta Davila. Source: Biblioteca de las Artes (Archivo CENIDIAP/INBA). Centro Nacional de las Artes. México.

Page 10: *Untitled* (study for the panel Germination, in the mural *A Hymn to the Earth*, Universidad Autómona de Chapingo, Mexico), 1926. Charcoal and pastel on paper, 24 ^{7}/8 in. x 19 in. San Francisco Museum of Modern Art, Albert M. Bender Collection, gift of Albert M. Bender. Photo by Don Myer.

Page 12: *Veiled Woman*, 1946. Oil on canvas, 60 in. x 48 in. Courtesy of Mary-Anne Martin/Fine Art, New York.

Page 15: *Mural Study of Hands, Chapingo*, 1927. Sanguine and charcoal on paper, 24 ^{3}/4 in. x 18 ^{3}/4 in. Courtesy of Mary-Anne Martin/Fine Art, New York.

Page 16: *Portrait of Dolores Olmeda*, 1955. Oil on canvas, 78 ^{3}/4 in. x 59 ^{13}/16 in. Fundacion Dolores Olmeda, Mexico City, D.F., Mexico. Credit: Schalkwijk/Art Resource, NY.

Page 19: *Portrait of Ruth Rivera*, 1949. Oil on canvas, 78 ^{3}/8 in. x 39 ^{3}/8 in. Colección: Rapael Coronel. Source: Biblioteca de las Artes (Archivo CENIDIAP/INBA). Centro Nacional de las Artes. México.

Pages 20–21: *Dance in Tehuantepec*, 1935. Charcoal and watercolor, 18 ^{3}/4 in. x 23 ^{3}/4 in. Los Angeles County Museum of Art. Gift of Mr. and Mrs. Milton W. Lipper from the Milton W. Lipper Estate. Copyright © 1999 Museum Associates, Los Angeles County Museum of Art. All Rights Reserved.

Page 23: *Washerwomen with Zopilotes*, 1928. Oil and encaustic on canvas, 22 in. x 16 ^{7}/8 in. Courtesy of Mary-Anne Martin/Fine Art, New York.

Page 24: *Untitled* (study for the mural *Allegory of California*), 1931. Pastel and charcoal on paper, 24 ^{1}/2 in. x 18 ^{7}/8 in. San Francisco Museum of Modern Art. Gift of William L. Gerstle through the San Francisco Art Institute.

Page 30: Photograph of Maya Angelou by Steve Dunwell.

Page 31: *Self-Portrait*, 1949. Tempera on linen, 13 ^{3}/4 in. x 11 in. Courtesy of Mary-Anne Martin/Fine Art, New York.